AMERIC...NS

STRUGGLES

Arvin Casas

Globe Fearon Educational Publisher
A Division of Simon & Schuster
Upper Saddle River, New Jersey

Project Editors: Keisha N. Carter, Lynn Kloss, Ann Clarkson
Poetry Writer and Editor: J.N. Fox
Director of Editorial and Marketing: Diane Galen
Executive Editor: Joan Carrafiello
Production Director: Kurt Scherwatzky
Production Editor: Alan Dalgleish
Marketing Manager: Margaret Rakus
Assistant Marketing Manager: Donna Frasco
Interior Electronic Design: Mimi Raihl
Art Direction: Armando Baez
Illustrator: Alan Nahigian
Electronic Page Production: Elaine Kilcullen and Mimi Raihl
Cover Design: Sheree Goodman Design
Cover Photo: Photo Credit

Photos: p. 9 The Bettman Archive; **p. 42** Archive Photos
Poetry: p.24 *Hoods* reprinted with permission of the author

Printed in the United States of America.
1 2 3 4 5 6 7 8 9 10   00 99 98 97 96

ISBN:0-8359-3359-8

GLOBE FEARON EDUCATIONAL PUBLISHER
A Division of Simon & Schuster
Upper Saddle River, New Jersey

Contents

To the Student

You are about to begin an adventure. Between the covers of this book are terrified hikers who discover an ancient world. There are people searching for life in outer space. There is love. There is courage. There is danger.

All the works focus on one theme: Struggles. The people in this book are facing difficult decisions. Should a young Native American run away from his pain? How can an escaped slave best help his people? Each person in this book has a different struggle to face.

Within this book are many different kinds of writing. There are short stories and profiles of people. There are interviews and news articles. There are entries from a diary, and letters. All of the selections show the many ways people express themselves.

When you read these works, notice how the writing differs. A diary often tells how a person is feeling. An interview shows you the point of view of the people who are talking. A series of letters may show you how someone feels at different times.

Above all, we hope you enjoy this book. Some of the people in these stories may have problems like yours. Some stories may help you think about what other people face in their lives. In one selection, you can imagine you must make a decision that will tear your family apart. In another selection, imagine how you would feel if you came to a new country— and learned you could not stay. Step into other people's shoes. Settle into this book and let your mind soar.

Before You Read
Through reading and writing, Frederick Douglass led a personal struggle against slavery in the United States.

The Power of Words: Frederick Douglass's Story

Frederick Douglass taught himself to read and write in a time when enslaved people were not allowed to read. Words allowed Frederick Douglass to free his mind and body. They allowed him to change his world. Because of him, many people learned firsthand how bad it was to be a slave. Words gave Frederick Douglass the power to help stop slavery in America.

Frederick Douglass was born enslaved, sometime in 1818, on a plantation in Maryland.

These were the days before The Civil War when many people in the U.S. enslaved Africans and African Americans to do all the hard work on their farms and homes.

At first, Frederick Douglass was called Frederick Bailey. Bailey was his mother's name. Although Frederick and his other brothers and sisters took the name Bailey, there was no real Bailey family. Slave owners did not allow enslaved people to have families. Slaves were thought of as property, not people. They were traded and sold.

So at the age of eight, Frederick was taken away from his family. He was forced to leave the only family and place he had ever known. Frederick was sold to the Auld family, who lived in the city of Baltimore, Maryland.

When he was older, Frederick realized that his new owner, Mrs. Auld, was new to owning slaves. He guessed that by the way she first treated him.

At first she was very kind to Frederick. Mrs. Auld clothed him and fed him well. This was much better than he had ever been treated on the plantation in Maryland. But although she was kind to him, she still kept him prisoner as her slave.

What was strange was that Mrs. Auld began to teach Frederick how to read. That gift would change his life.

Other slave owners believed that enslaved people could not learn. Many slave owners were afraid to let enslaved people learn how to read. They knew that if enslaved people knew how to read and write, slave owners might not be able to control them anymore.

Slave owners always tried to keep the people they enslaved from thinking about freedom. Slave owners feared anything that would make enslaved people free thinkers. Free thinkers would always want to be free people.

But Mrs. Auld did not know the effects of learning to read. She taught young Frederick the ABCs. Frederick learned them quickly and soon began to read by himself.

When Mr. Auld found out that his wife had been teaching Frederick to read, he became very angry with her. He made her stop.

Although Mr. Auld was able to make his wife stop, it was already too late. She had already given Frederick a gift and a tool that could never be taken away from him. Frederick had learned to read. It marked the beginning of his search for freedom.

Even though slave owners thought that enslaved people couldn't learn to read, Frederick Douglass proved them wrong. If slave owners were wrong about him, what else were they wrong about, wondered Frederick. He knew he had to learn more. Frederick had to try to learn by himself. Since it was illegal, Frederick had to be very sneaky.

Wherever and whenever he could, Frederick Douglass read. He hid and read old newspapers that he found on the street. Sometimes, he tricked some of the young white children he played with to teach him how to read. He even borrowed their school books and practiced reading and writing by himself.

When he had to run errands for Mrs. Auld, he went to the shipyards in Baltimore. There he watched and copied the boat builders. Some of the men would write in notebooks on their lunch breaks, others would read a book. That was one of the many places young Frederick Douglass learned to read and write.

But sometimes Frederick got caught and got into trouble. Mrs. Auld had changed by then. She had been kind at first, but then she became very mean. She could not make Frederick forget how to read, but she did everything she could to stop him.

Whenever she caught Frederick reading, she punished him. This really surprised Frederick. He began to understand how wrong slavery was and how it changed people.

The change in Mrs. Auld taught Frederick Douglass many lessons. He had already realized that reading was an important and powerful skill. He could tell that by how others tried to stop him.

Frederick also began to realize how evil slavery was. Slavery could change people. Slavery changed kind people into angry, hateful ones. He saw that in Mrs. Auld. Slavery was bad for both enslaved people and slave owners.

But slavery was also evil because it kept enslaved people as prisoners. By keeping enslaved people away from books and education, they could be kept from learning. Frederick realized that slavery kept people and their minds prisoners.

But Frederick had escaped, at least in his mind. Through reading, his thoughts began to grow. His mind became free. Reading opened Frederick Douglass's eyes and let him see how wrong slavery really was.

One of the school books he borrowed from the white children was old. It talked about how wrong slavery was. The book was an ancient story about an intelligent slave arguing with his master about why slavery was bad. Frederick could relate to this story. Frederick began to realize that, if slavery was wrong hundreds of years ago, it was still wrong now. If many white people read and knew this, why did they still enslave others?

The more he read, the more he began to hate how he and other African Americans were forced to be prisoners. He began to see slavery as a crime against people. The more reading he did the more freed his mind became and, the more he became angry. But he also became very sad. With a free mind he realized more and more each day that his body was still trapped in slavery. He wanted to die.

One day Frederick read a newspaper article about people trying to end slavery. This surprised him. There was always a rumor about people trying to end slavery. Until he had read it in the newspaper, he had never believed the rumor. Frederick did everything he could to read and find out more about these people.

FREDERICK DOUGLASS   9

When Frederick read about these people, he realized that he was not alone. He began to see that he was not the only person who did not like slavery. He saw that others also thought slavery was evil. He began to feel less sad about being enslaved. He began to hope. He began to see that there really was a chance he could be free.

Frederick Douglass learned that the people who were trying to end slavery were called abolitionists. Many of them lived in the North. Slavery had ended in the North many years before. There were even free African American abolitionists in the North, working to end slavery, too.

Many abolitionists were trying to end slavery in the South. Some had even come down South. They wrote letters and articles and made speeches against slavery. Many of them were put in jail. None of the Southern slave owners wanted to let their slaves go.

Many abolitionists did what they could to stop slavery. They even helped some slaves escape North. Because of this, many Southerners treated abolitionists as criminals. To them, abolitionists were thieves.

When Frederick Douglass read about the abolitionists, he felt as if he had finally found people on his side. If abolitionists were criminals just because they wanted to free enslaved people, Frederick saw again how that proved slavery was evil. How could people doing good things be criminals? How could freedom be bad?

For now, Frederick Douglass could only dream about running away to freedom. But the more he read about freedom, the more he wanted it.

Frederick began to understand why the Aulds did not want him to read. An education could be a dangerous weapon against slavery. That's why they kept it away from enslaved people. Frederick realized how lucky he was to know how to read.

The slave owners knew that an education could be a powerful tool. They believed that teaching slaves to read and write was dangerous. If a slave could read, a slave might find out how wrong slavery really was, just as Frederick had.

Frederick had cheated the odds. He had stolen the tool and weapon of words. He had learned to do what he wasn't allowed to do. His body might have been enslaved, but knowing how to read freed his mind. Soon nothing could stop him from wanting freedom for all enslaved people.

That was the beginning for the man we now know as Frederick Douglass. He spent a few more years growing up in Baltimore. For a short time, he was sold to another master. Because he knew how to read, it was hard for people to enslave Frederick. As his mind became more and more free, he hated slavery more and more. He understood, perhaps more than they did, why slavery was wrong.

Because he was hard to enslave, Frederick was traded back to the Aulds in Baltimore. During that time, Frederick met the woman who would later become his wife. Although she was African American, she was not enslaved. She was free. She had come from the free North. Frederick was amazed by her. He fell in love with her and her freedom. When she went back North, Frederick knew he had to escape.

Frederick waited for the right time. Years later, in 1838, he escaped. By pretending to be a freeman sailor, he was able to make his way up North. It was a very dangerous escape, but he made it.

He met his wife again and they married. Frederick then changed his last name to Douglass. With a different name, it would be harder to find him and return him to the South.

But freedom was not the end for Frederick Douglass. Even though he was free, millions of others in the South were still enslaved. He still felt the need to fight against slavery. He had fought it for himself. Now he knew he needed to fight for others. Because he had the powerful tool of reading and writing in his grasp, Frederick decided to use it against slavery.

Frederick joined the abolitionists he had read about years before. Because he had taught himself to read and write, he knew he would be a powerful fighter against slavery. Because he had actually been a slave, he could better tell people about how horrible it really was.

Many Northerners were impressed by his words and his story. He had learned to read and write so well that he could speak better than many other educated people. His skill made him hard to ignore. Never before had people heard a firsthand account of slavery spoken so well.

Now that Frederick was free to speak out against the evils of slavery, nothing was going to slow him down. Frederick refused to close his mind again. He wrote many best-selling books about his life as a slave. Because he used the real names of his former owners, he had to leave the country for two years. Even though he was free in the North, there was always the risk he could be arrested and taken back South. However, in 1847, English friends bought Frederick Douglass's freedom. He returned to the United States, a free man forever.

Nothing could make Frederick Douglass stop.

His books and speeches made him a very wealthy man. Even with his great success, Frederick Douglass continued to risk everything, even his freedom, to fight to end slavery. He knew he had to succeed at all costs.

Frederick showed others how wrong it was to keep free-thinking people enslaved. He showed people how wrong it was to force people to stay in the dark. He had seen personally how slavery made people evil. Now that both his mind and body were free, it was his duty to do all he could to bring slavery to an end.

Just by knowing how to read, Frederick Douglass helped in the fight to stop slavery. If it hadn't been for the power of words, Frederick Douglass would have never been able to help end one of the cruelest injustices in our history.

Think About It

1. How did Frederick Douglass learn to read?

2. Why was it illegal for slaves to read?

3. Imagine you are Frederick Douglass. Like him, you have the gift of words. What would you tell people about slavery?

Before You Read
Sometimes the biggest struggle
in life is letting go and saying
good-bye.

The Palace

March 11

I had a great birthday today. Grandmother came by early in the day and took me to a big old movie theater downtown called the Palace Theater. They show old movies in there, I thought. I also thought I wouldn't like them, but some of them were really funny. I laughed so hard my stomach still hurts.

What I liked best, though, was the theater itself. The building is very nice. I was really more interested in the building than in the movies. I think it was because Grandma had told me so many great stories about the place.

Even though the Palace Theater is old and starting to fall apart, it must have been a very beautiful place years ago. It still looks nice now. A little paint here and there would help make it look new. Grandma says it needs "spit and polish."

I've never seen anything like the Palace before, it's just the best. It is much bigger than any movie theater I have ever been to.

The ones near where Mom and I live are different. They are cinemas. The buildings are big, but they have lots of small theaters inside. They show all the new movies. They show so many movies at the same time, that it's sometimes hard to pick which one to see.

The old theaters were different. They all used to be like the Palace, said Grandma. Many of them are gone now, because the new cinemas make more money.

But unlike the new movie theaters, the old theater is *huge*! There is only one screen in the whole building. The screen is very wide. They can only show one movie at a time. There are hundreds of seats. They even have a balcony so they can fit more people in the theater. Too bad they only show old movies, one at a time.

Someone must have spent a lot of time decorating the theater. The walls have many paintings on them. There are really big red velvet curtains on each side of the screen. The ceiling has gold paint and even more paintings on it. The whole place is filled with colorful decorations and other frilly things. The seats are a little creaky, but they are soft and very comfortable. I felt like I was sitting in a palace.

My grandmother said she used to work in the Palace years ago. She wore a funny uniform. When we got back home she showed me a picture of herself in the theater. Grandmother was young and pretty in her uniform. She had a flashlight and a funny hat. She almost looked like a soldier.

But she wasn't. Her job was to help people find seats in the dark. In the old days, movies would show over and over again without a pause. You could come in at any time. For a few cents you could go inside in the morning and leave late at night. There was always a movie showing. It was always dark. You could see the same movie over and over again if you wanted.

Grandma said she saw lots of movies when she worked there. She saw some so many times that she memorized them. She acted a few lines from some of those movies for me. I had never heard of any of the movies. She said many of the old movies had songs in them, and she sang one to me. I think Grandma secretly wished she was a movie star.

Grandma told me that she first met Grandpa at the Palace Theater. They met one day when there was a big Hollywood premiere. Lots of famous movie stars came to see the film open there. I asked Grandma which stars she saw that night. I had never even heard of most of them. Grandma tells me that they were very famous, so I believe her. I said that a big theater like that seemed like the right place for famous movie stars. Grandma agreed.

Grandma told me how Grandpa had come from across the city to the theater to see the movie stars that night. The place was crowded with fans, but he tried to sneak in. Grandma caught him, but for some reason she didn't kick him out. She said he had a lucky face, so she found him a seat up in the balcony, way in the back.

I thought a seat in the back would be bad. But Grandma took me up there. I saw that even though it was way in the back, you could still see the movie. The screen is so big, you can see it from every seat. No seat in the Palace was a bad seat.

Grandma told me how often she and Grandpa sat and watched the movie together. I can't remember what movie it was, but I remember it was a really good movie. People call it a classic now. I think I saw part of it on TV once. Grandma says it was much better to watch at the Palace. I believe her.

Even after the movie stars left that first night, Grandma and Grandpa stayed. They watched the movie again and again. Grandma says it was because they also liked the seats. Those seats became their favorite and regular place to sit.

Everytime Grandpa came to see the movies he sat with her in those seats. Even though he lived on the other side of the city, he always came to watch movies at that theater with Grandma. I think he came to see her, too.

Grandma let me sit in Grandpa's chair. She says I have his lucky face.

Grandpa asked Grandma to marry her in those seats. Grandma said it was all like a movie. Of course, I said, they spent so much time at the movies. No wonder Grandma still loves that theater. She loves their favorite seats.

The next time Grandma visits, we're going to go back there. I wish I could go by myself, but Mom won't allow me to go into the city without a grown-up yet. Mom doesn't have time for us to go all that way for a movie. But Grandma does. I can't wait to go there again.

April 20

. . . Grandma and I went back to the movie theater. We sat in Grandpa's and Grandma's seats again. She said they were ours now. Grandpa died years ago. Grandma said she was taking care of their seats. I promised her that I would take care of our seats even after she was gone. Grandma cried. I don't think it was the movie that made her cry. . . .

May 18

. . . Grandma and I went to the Palace again. We've been going almost every week now. I think it is a special place. . . .

May 30

. . . Grandma and I were supposed to go to the Palace today, but she said she was feeling tired. Grandma seems to be feeling tired a lot lately. I hope she is OK. I can't wait to see the Palace again. . . .

June 12

Grandma is staying with us now. She is in bed and is very sick. Mom is very sad. I am, too. Grandma doesn't like us to feel sad. She made Mom let me go into town and go to the Palace. She wanted me to go and sit in our seats. She wanted me to be happy. She said it would make her happy if I went. Mom said it was OK.

I was a little nervous about going. But I did it. It's not that hard a trip because the Palace is right near the train station. I was surprised Mom let me go, though. I guess I'm getting old enough to do things on my own.

July 4

Today is the 4th of July, but I don't feel like celebrating. Grandma died a few days ago. We buried her today at the cemetery right next to Grandpa. Tomorrow Mom and I are going to the Palace to see a movie. I promised Grandma I would take Mom. Right now I don't feel like going to the Palace, but I made a promise to take care of our seats.

Jul y 5

. . . we went to the Palace. They were showing one of the old movies Grandma used to know all the words from. Even though it was a funny movie, Mom and I cried. We sat in our special seats. . . .

September 22

School is getting busy now. The sixth grade seems much harder than the fifth. They give us much more homework. I don't have time to visit the Palace as much as I would like to. I hope to be able to go again by Thanksgiving.

November 22

. . . I was finally able to go the Palace today. I sat in our seats. It was really cold in the theater, though. I asked the man who sold me a ticket why it was cold. He said because they didn't have enough money to heat the Palace anymore. I said I would bring a thicker coat the next time I came. He laughed. . . .

December 18

I was able to go into town again today and visit the Palace. There were no movies showing, which was weird. I peeked inside the windows on one of the doors. The Palace looked empty. Maybe they're fixing the heat.

January 30

Mom gave me a newspaper article today. When I read it, I got very angry. The newspaper said that someone had bought the Palace. At first I thought that was good. I hoped they would fix it up and make it warm. But I read that the people who bought the Palace were going to tear it down. They said they were going to make it into a parking lot. I asked Mom if they could do that. She said if they owned it, they could do anything. All I can think is, What would Grandma think? I wonder what she would do. I bet she would be as angry as I am.

February 15

I snuck out of school today and took the train into town to see the Palace. I stood outside the doors. Signs were put up saying they would tear it down in March. I felt very sad.

On another door, someone had put up a flyer. Someone had started a group to try and stop the new owners from tearing down the Palace. They called the Palace a historical landmark. The flyer said they were holding meetings to organize a protest to save the Palace Theater.

I think I'm going to go. They said they needed as much help as they could get in order to save the Palace. I'm definitely going to go and help. I can't make any of the meetings except the very last one. I'm going to have to sneak out of school again for it.

February 22

Today was a big day. I went to the meeting to save the Palace today. It was at a coffee shop near the theater. The people there were surprised to see me in the coffee shop. They were a lot older than I was. Most of them were as old as Grandma. One old man tried to offer me some coffee. I said I didn't drink coffee, and they all laughed.

There were really only about ten people there. Only ten people cared about the Palace. I can't believe it, I thought everyone would love that theater.

We sat in a circle and talked about the Palace. When it was my turn, I told my story about Grandpa and Grandma. Everyone smiled. One lady said she knew my Grandma! She had worked with her all those years ago. She had worn the same funny hat and uniform.

Someone said that they had tried talking to the new owners of the Palace. The new owners refused to stop their plans. Another person said that they had tried to talk to the Historical Society, but even they couldn't help. Everyone sighed.

I asked the old woman who had known Grandma what the Historical Society was all about. She told me that if a building was an important building in history, you couldn't tear it down. Like George Washington's or Lincoln's house. I said I thought the Palace was important. I said Grandma and Grandpa thought it was important, too. Wasn't that history?

The woman agreed with me. But she said that because the historical people didn't think so, there was nothing we could do to stop the new owners. It would become a parking lot. One of the people at the meeting was a college student. He suggested that we chain ourselves to the Palace to stop the bulldozers. The older people laughed at him.

I was mad that they laughed at him. I thought it was a weird idea, too, but didn't they want to save the Palace? I got up and told them about how I had made a promise to my Grandma. I talked about our seats. The only thing the group could do was nod their heads and sigh.

When the meeting was over, I was mad at them. Were they giving up? I asked the old woman. She said with a small tear in her eye that sometimes we have to let go of things. I didn't listen to her. I ran out and caught the train home.

Mom found out I had skipped out of school early. She was mad. I tried to explain, but she grounded me. I'm not allowed out of the house for two weeks, except for school!

March 3

Even though I was still grounded, I didn't go to school today. I went downtown instead to say good-bye to the Palace. I watched as the bulldozers lined up. I cried as the wrecking ball smashed the side of that old beautiful building. I watched the workers chase the college student away from the bulldozers.

I could see inside through the hole in the wall. I could see up in the balcony. Even though I was standing on the other side of the street, behind the barriers the workers had put up, I could see it all. I thought this must have been the view the people on the screen had of the people in the seats.

I looked as hard as I could. As the dust lifted for a brief second, I saw our special seats for the last time.

I thought for a second I saw Mom there, standing on the other side of the street. I couldn't tell though, because I couldn't see through the dust.

I cried on the train ride home. . . .

March 11

Today was my birthday. It was only a year ago that Grandma first brought me to the Palace. When I remembered that I was sad.

But when I went downstairs for breakfast, mother had a surprise for me. In the living room were two seats from the Palace! I had seen her there! Mom said that they were Grandma's seats.

I don't know how, but somehow she was able to save them from the Palace. Mom said they were important to her as well. They were important to our whole family, so she couldn't let them go. Although we couldn't save the Palace, at least we could save the seats, she said.

I still feel bad about losing the Palace, but Mom says that's the way life goes sometimes. But having the seats makes me feel a little better. Mom says I can keep them in my room. They will make a neat sofa.

Think About It

1. Why is the Palace so important to the writer's grandmother?

2. How does the Palace differ from modern movie cinemas?

3. Have you ever had a favorite thing that you had to give up? Write about it and how you felt.

Before You Read
The street can be a dangerous place. In this poem, the narrator escaped when he is chased by a group of bullies.

Hoods

Paul B. Janeczko

In black leather jackets,
watching Spider work
the wire coat hanger
into Mrs. Koop's car,
they reminded me of crows
huddled around a road kill.
Startled,
they looked up' then back
at Spider,
who nodded once,
setting them free
toward me.

I bounded away,
used a parking meter
to whip me around the corner
past Janelli's Market,
the darkened Pine Street Grille,
and the steamed windows
of Sudsy's Modern Laundromat.

I climbed—two at a time—
the granite steps
of the Free Public Library
and pushed back thick wooden doors
as the pursuing pack stopped—
sinners at the door of a church.

From the corner table of the reference room
I watched them
pacing,
heads turning every time the door opened,
pacing
until Spider arrived
to draw them away.

I waited,
fingering hearts,
initials carved into the table,
grinning as I heard myself telling Raymond
of my death-defying escape.

Think About It

1. Why did the group of bullies chase the narrator?
2. Why is the narrator grinning at the end of the poem?
3. Have you had an experience with a group of bullies? Explain.

Before You Read

One of the rights Americans have is the right to free speech. But should we really be allowed to say whatever we want to? The following is a short play about a problem of free speech.

A Play on Words

TALK SHOW HOST: (*to the audience*) Hello, ladies and gentlemen. Today we'll be talking about free speech on our show . In some parts of the world, you can go to jail for saying things other people don't like. Some books, movies, and TV shows are banned because people don't like them. Here in the United States, we are lucky. One of our basic and most important rights as citizens is that we can say, read, and watch whatever we want to. But how far should we take this right? Do we have the right to say or show anything? For example, is it OK for songs and books to use bad words? Is it OK for TV shows and movies to show violence?

Today we are going to hear from two people who disagree about how far the right to free speech should be taken. Our first guest is Doris Wall. She is a working mother with three children. After school, her children are alone for two or three hours a day until Doris comes home from work. One day Doris came home and found her kids watching a violent movie on television. She was so upset that she started a group that works to stop violence on TV.

Our second guest is also a working mother. Her name is Arlene Whittaker and she has two boys. Unlike Doris, Arlene thinks that TV stations should show whatever they want. She thinks it's up to parents to control what their kids watch on TV.

We will hear from Doris first. Hello, Doris.

DORIS: Hello.

HOST: Tell us what happened.

DORIS: Well, as you said, I am a working mother. I work until five o'clock as a secretary. My kids usually come home from school before I do. Sometimes they watch TV before I come home.

HOST: How old are your children?

DORIS: I have three children. My two girls are eight and nine years old. I also have a boy who is twelve.

HOST: They are young.

DORIS: Yes they are.

HOST: You must have been shocked when you found them watching a violent movie on TV.

DORIS: Yes, I was. I don't mind it when my kids watch TV. There are many other nice shows. Many are good for kids to see.

HOST: But this movie was different?

DORIS: Oh yes! It was very violent. When I opened the door to our house, I saw them watching it.

HOST: What was wrong with the movie?

DORIS: Oh my! It was so violent! The movie had car crashes. It showed people getting shot. People were fighting and cursing. It showed lots of blood.

HOST: So what did you do?

DORIS: I rushed over to the television. I turned it off. I was very mad.

HOST: Were you mad at your kids?

DORIS: Yes, but I was more angry at the people who put that movie on television. I don't want my kids seeing such bad things.

HOST: I can understand that. What did you do after that?

DORIS: After my kids ate dinner and I put them to bed, I started thinking about that movie. I thought there should be a law against showing those kinds of things on TV. But I felt like I couldn't do anything about it. That's when I called up my friend. She is a mother, too. We started talking about all the bad things kids see on TV. We decided to start a group to stop it.

HOST: What kind of group?

DORIS: We are a group of concerned mothers. We go to TV stations and try to make them stop showing these violent movies.

HOST: What did the TV people think of you?

DORIS: Many were rude to us. They said it was their right to show whatever they wanted to.

HOST: Really? What did you do then?

DORIS: Well, many of us went down to the TV station again. We formed a line in the lobby. We said we wouldn't leave unless they stopped showing violent movies. We also contacted the station's advertisers. We said we would stop buying their products if they advertised during the violent shows.

HOST: Did that stop them?

DORIS: Yes. After a few days, they stopped.

HOST: Wow! So in one way, you now control what's on that TV station!

DORIS: Yes.

HOST: That's very interesting. So I guess now you'll try to keep all violent movies off TV?

DORIS: Yes.

HOST: That brings us to our second guest, Arlene Whittaker. She is another mother. Like Doris, she does not like violence on TV. But she does not like what Doris and her group are doing. (*To Arlene*) Welcome, Arlene.

ARLENE: Thank you for having me on your show.

HOST: Well, we've just heard about Doris and her group. It sounds like they are trying to do a good thing. Tell us, why do you think they are doing a bad thing?

ARLENE: First, let me say that I am a mother, too. I have two boys. They are eight and ten.

DORIS: They are almost the same age as my children.

ARLENE: Yes. Like Doris, I do not like my boys watching violent movies on TV.

HOST: But you don't agree with what Doris is doing?

ARLENE: No.

HOST: Why not?

ARLENE: It is one thing to be concerned about what is on TV. It is OK to control what things your children can watch. I do it myself. But it is dangerous when you start telling other people what they are allowed to see.

HOST: Dangerous? Why is it dangerous? It sounds like they are just trying to protect children.

ARLENE: Protecting *children* from violent shows isn't

dangerous. You should protect your children. I think every parent must do that. But what Doris is doing is different. She is forcing other people to watch the things that only she likes. She is not letting them have the freedom to choose what they want to see. That's what is dangerous.

HOST: I see. You mention the word "freedom." What do you mean?

ARLENE: In this country we have certain freedoms. One of them is the right to free speech. That doesn't just mean you can say whatever you want to. It also means you can see or listen to whatever you choose. It is a right of everyone to think for yourself. This right is part of what makes us Americans.

HOST: But why is what Doris is doing dangerous?

ARLENE: It is dangerous because what she is doing is getting in the way of free speech. She is forcing TV stations to show us what her group says is OK.

DORIS: What's wrong with that?

ARLENE: Plenty. By stopping the TV station from showing what they want to, you are getting in the way of their right to free speech. When you stop movies just because *you* don't like them, you are getting in the way of our right to hear or see what we want. This is called censorship.

HOST: We hear this word all the time. What is censorship?

ARLENE: Censorship is when our right to free speech is blocked. It is when books, information, movies, or TV shows are blocked by other people just because they don't like them.

DORIS: But what about violence on TV? Do TV stations have a right to show ugly things to our children? I think that's dangerous.

ARLENE: Even though we may not like everything TV stations show, they have the right to show those things.

DORIS: But you are a mother, too. Do you want your children watching those bad things? Why do you let your children see these evil movies?

ARLENE: I don't. I turn the TV off.

DORIS: How is that different from what I am doing?

ARLENE: As I said, I turn off *my* TV. I do not tell the TV station what to say or do. Other people watch TV besides our children. Maybe they want to watch those kinds of movies. Our rights as Americans allow us to watch what movies we want to see. You don't have the right to stop other people. You can turn off the TV in your own home. You can't go to everyone's house and turn off their TVs.

DORIS: I don't do that.

ARLENE: But in a way you do. You are blocking the rights of others to watch what they want to.

DORIS: But what about my rights? I have to work hard all day. I can't be at home all the time to turn off the TV.

Don't I have a right to control what shows are on? Don't I have a right to protect my children?

ARLENE: You have every right to protect your children, but you don't have the right to protect other people. They are not your children.

HOST: That's a very interesting problem. On one hand we have the right to say or think about what we want to. But on the other hand, do we have the right to force what we think on other people?

ARLENE: No we don't.

DORIS: But what about those TV stations? Aren't they forcing me to see what they want me or my kids to see? What about my rights to think what I want to think. What about my rights to see what I want to see. What about my rights to do what I want to do.

ARLENE: You have the right to control your life, and your own home, and your own children. Why not do what I do? Make a rule. No TV until Mom gets home. That way you can watch TV with your children You can then turn it off, or change the channel when bad things come on.

DORIS: When I'm not at home, how do I know my children will follow the rule?

ARLENE: Since you can't control the TV in your own house, is that why you are trying to control the TV station?

DORIS: Yes.

ARLENE: TV stations should not replace your job as a mother. If you can't control what your kids do, you shouldn't try to control others. You shouldn't try to control the TV stations or anybody else!

DORIS: All I'm trying to do is protect my kids!

ARLENE: All I'm trying to do is protect my country and the rights of every citizen!

HOST: Now, now. Let's calm down here. As you people in the audience can see, this is a pretty hot subject. What should we do as concerned people? What can we do? Doris?

DORIS: Yes?

HOST: I understand your point. I understand what you are trying to do. I am a father myself. But sometimes, when my children are asleep, I don't mind watching some of those violent movies. I think I am old enough to handle them.

DORIS: But not everyone out there is. Children should not be allowed to see such violence.

HOST: Yes, I understand that. But in a way, you're not allowing me to see them either.

DORIS: Maybe you shouldn't see them.

HOST: But what if I choose to? Isn't that up to me?

DORIS: Yes.

HOST: But aren't you and your group now choosing

for me? (*to Arlene*) Arlene, isn't this the censorship you were talking about?

ARLENE: Yes! I don't like violent movies myself, but I respect your right to watch them if you want to. I would never force the TV stations to stop showing them just because I don't like them.

DORIS: You're crazy!

ARLENE: Where does it all stop? Sure, we all want to be comfortable when we watch TV. We change channels to watch things we like. We change channels when there are things we don't like. Sometimes, I just turn the TV off. But is it really right to make other people watch only what we like? Does our right to say what we want to mean we have the right to force people to listen to us?

DORIS: But that's what the TV stations are doing! They are forcing us see those violent movies!

HOST: Wait now. Let's calm down again Doris, who is forcing you to watch these movies?

DORIS: The TV stations.

HOST: When I listen to the radio, or I'm watching TV and something comes on I don't like, I just change stations.

ARLENE: Or you can just turn it off.

HOST: Yes. That's true. I like to read a good book, too. But what I want to ask Doris is, who is forcing you to watch these things?

DORIS: The TV stations are forcing me. They show them without asking if we really want to see them. I have a right to speak up if I think a station is doing a bad thing, don't I?

ARLENE: Yes, you have the right to say so.

DORIS: Exactly. All I'm trying to do is make sure that there is at least one TV station in our town that I can watch and not feel shocked. Don't people like me and my group have a right to have a choice? Don't we have a right to have a TV station that represents us?

ARLENE: Sure you do.

HOST: Hmmm. What do you do when someone like Doris can't find a TV station that speaks for her?

DORIS: You make a TV station do what you want it to do. You use your right to speak out against things you don't like. You have a right to try and make your world a better place. Just like my group did.

HOST: Ah, I see we are back to the beginning again. It's a very complicated issue, isn't it? It looks like this problem over our right to free speech isn't going to go away.

ARLENE: I don't think the problem should go away. It's good for people to discuss the issues.

DORIS: I agree with that.

HOST: Maybe someday we'll solve it. But I'm afraid not today. It looks like we're out of time for today.

draw the line on free speech? Is censorship ever OK? Exercise your own right to speak your mind and write us about what you think. (*To Doris*) Thank you for coming here today, Doris.

DORIS: Thank you.

HOST: (*To Arlene*) Thank you too, Arlene.

ARLENE: Thank you.

HOST: And thank you all for watching the show today. See you again tomorrow!

Think About It

1. What is Doris's position on free speech? Why does she want to ban violent movies on TV?

2. What is Arlene's position on free speech? Why does she think censorship is wrong?

3. Who do you believe is right, Doris or Arlene? Why?

Sometimes people don't even know who they are. In the following story, a teenaged boy struggles to define himself.

Running Away

John Williams never had to tell anyone that he was part Native American. People always seemed to guess it. Though you couldn't tell by the sound of his name or by the way he acted, white people said they could tell. They knew John was "Indian" by the way he looks. This always bothered John.

John was half white and half Navajo. It was something he always thought about. When he saw Native Americans from the Reservation, they reminded him of his Navajo blood. When he saw white people in the town and at school, they reminded him, too.

It seemed that no matter where he went, John felt he was different. People didn't have to tell him. He felt it himself.

John had never met his white father. But he knew the story. His father had been one of the few white people who worked in the coal mines on the Navajo Reservation.

Many years ago, the United States government had forced the Navajo Indians off their land. They were made to live in a separate area called a reservation. Many Navajo lived and worked on the Reservation. It was like their own country.

But the Navajo people did not get much money or help from the government. The Reservation was not as nice as other places in the state. Some parts of it did not have running water, or good electricity. In some parts the roads were very bad. Many of the people who lived there were poor.

One of the ways the people on the Navajo Reservation tried to make money was to work in the coal mines. The mines were on the Reservation, and many Navajo worked in them. Some white people also came to work in the mines. John's father was one of them.

Because life on the Reservation was hard, many Navajo people left. They moved to the many local towns that were near the Reservation. These were called border towns. All kinds of different people lived in these towns. Some were Navajo. Some were Mexican Americans. Some were white. John's father was one of the white people from one of the border towns.

Even though some left, some Navajo preferred to live on the Reservation. John's grandfather had a sheep farm there. Though he did not make a lot of money, it was enough to live on the Reservation.

John's mother also used to live on the Reservation. She had grown up there. As a teenager, she was young, pretty, and smart. She did not like living on the Reservation. She wanted to move away. She wanted to live in a place that was more modern. But she was still too young, so she lived with John's grandfather. She helped him with his sheep.

One day, years before John was born, his mother was herding her father's sheep. She was walking near the mining road, and a truck slowly drove by. It was filled with men from the mines, going home to the border town.

John's mother first saw his father on that truck. He was sitting in the back of the pickup with the other miners.

She thought he was very handsome. As they passed her, John's father waved at her. When he smiled at her, she blushed.

From then on, John's mother made it a habit to take her sheep by that road everyday. She would always wait to see the miners' trucks going by. She hoped to see the handsome man again.

One day she was walking by herself on the road. Her father didn't need her to take the sheep out that day, she went by herself. A truck stopped beside her. John's father was inside. He offered her a ride. After spending time together, they fell in love.

John's father wanted his mother to live with him. She didn't mind. She would be happy to leave the Reservation and move to the border town. He said he had a small house with electricity that they could share. He even had a big television.

John's grandfather did not want her to go. He did not like the miner. He thought he was a bad man. He wanted his daughter to stay with him on the Reservation. He did not want her to leave her family and her people.

But she ran away with the miner. They lived together for a few years. John was born. After that, John's father stopped working at the Navajo mine. He found a job driving a truck. John's mother stayed at home. She watched the big TV and raised John.

One day John's father climbed into his truck. He drove away and never came back. John was left all alone with his mother.

John's mother had to sell their house and the big TV. She didn't want to go home to the Reservation. She was still angry with her father. She got a job as a waitress at a nearby truck stop. Many truck drivers ate there.

Maybe, she hoped, one of them would know about John's father.

After his father left, John's mother stopped talking about him. That's why John never knew his father's whole name. All he knew was that his father was white, and that his last name was Williams. All John knew was the story his mother had told him.

After his father left, John lived in the small apartment he and his mother were able to find in the border town. It was in a poor neighborhood where other Navajo lived. Sometimes, when he was young, his mother left him with the neighbors when she had to work. Other times, when she had to work long hours, she had him stay with his grandfather on the Reservation.

When he was younger, John did not mind staying with his grandfather. The Reservation was a different world. They didn't have any televisions in his grandfather's house. His grandfather didn't like TV. His grandfather blamed the TV and other modern machines for John's mother's leaving him.

John sometimes helped his grandfather. They walked together, herding the sheep. John even helped his grandfather sell the sheep wool to the rug makers on the Reservation. When John stayed with his grandfather he met other Navajo. They seemed poorer than the Navajo in the border town. John asked his grandfather why he didn't want to move to the nicer border town. His grandfather said he liked living on the Reservation better. He liked it because it was simpler. He liked the Navajo traditions on the Reservation.

During the times he walked with his grandfather, John sometimes asked about his father. He hoped that he could learn more about him. But John's grandfather never talked about John's father. He would get a sad and angry look on his face. It was the same face he made whenever John's mother took John back to the border town.

When John was a little older, his mother stopped working at the truck stop. She got a much nicer job in a bank. She got a lot more money. They moved out of the poor Navajo neighborhood in the border town. They moved to another apartment on the other side of town, where mostly white people lived. They were able to buy their own big TV.

In the new neighborhood, John really grew up. His mother had more money now. John was old enough to stay in the apartment by himself. He didn't have to go to the Reservation anymore. Soon his grandfather and the Reservation were only memories to him.

Since they lived in a white neighborhood, most of his classmates were white. It was at school that John started to realize that he was different.

The white kids used to tease him. They called him names and made fun of him because he was Navajo. They said he should go back to the Reservation. John sometimes cried because they teased him so much.

When John cried, his mother comforted him. She would tell him the story of his father. She would remind him that he was also half white. She said that they would never go back to the Reservation. This made John feel better. It made him feel like he belonged with the white kids.

As he got older, John stopped crying so much. He began to act more and more like the white kids. He did everything he could to make them forget that he was part Navajo. He tried as hard as he could to bring out his white half.

John always talked about his white father. But the one story he knew about his father was not enough.

John began to lie about his father. He made up many lies to impress the white kids. He said his father was a rich man and was coming back for him. He sometimes said his father was a war hero—a soldier who had died overseas. Sometimes his stories were so good that he began to believe them himself.

Many white kids accepted John as a friend. Others did not. Some kids would play with him and became friends with him. But others still only saw John as a Navajo and they refused to be friends with any Navajo.

To them, John was only half white. That's why John hated it when white people could only see him as a Navajo. He had become as white as any of them. But they could only see his Navajo side.

When John was older and started going to high school, he still hated being half Navajo. Though at that point people didn't tease him anymore. He could still tell when being Navajo worked against him.

As before, some white people liked him and some didn't. There were always certain parties John could go to. However there were some that he could not go to.

Many of John's white friends didn't care that he was part Navajo. It was just the other kids who did care. Those were the cool kids in high school. John wanted them to like him. He secretly wanted to be as cool as those white kids were.

John worked hard to become popular. He wanted all the white people to like him. He wanted them to accept him as one of their own. John started joining clubs and staying after school so he could try and impress the cool kids.

He did well in sports. It came easily to him. But he hated it when people assumed he was good because he was Navajo.

He tried other activities, other clubs, and did well there, too. He was as smart as his mother. He did well in school. He was very good in math and in English class.

But the same people who said he was good at sports because he was Navajo never accepted it when John did well in class. They would congratulate him, but they would always point out how weird it was for him to be so intelligent. They thought it was weird only because he was Navajo.

It seemed that no matter what he did, no matter what success he had, he would have to be measured against other Navajo.

There were a few other Navajo people in his school. John didn't care for them. He could only guess that they hated him, too. He made fun of them much more than any white kids did. Often he found himself calling them names, forgetting who he was. When his friends reminded him that he was Navajo too, John got angry at them.

Sometimes they would see other Navajo, outside of school. This was rare, because most Navajo lived on the other side of town, where John and his mother used to live.

Sometimes when they walked home from school, they would find a poor homeless Navajo sleeping in the street. Everyone knew that these Navajo were from the Reservation. The homeless Navajo were a joke to the white kids. They embarrassed John. He yelled and cursed at the homeless men.

"Go back to the Reservation!" John yelled.

When his white friends reminded him that he was also Navajo, he would get embarrassed. During these times he hated the Navajo, and the Navajo in himself, the most.

One day John stayed late after school. John had run in a track meet, and had won the race. Even though he was tired, John was very happy. Some of the cool white kids in his class had even cheered for him. One even shook his hand.

John was very proud. He was always happy when others cheered for him. He liked it the most when it was the cool white kids. John even got a medal. He wore it around his neck as he walked home alone.

When John was only a few blocks from school, a truck pulled up behind him. Some of the rich, cool white kids were in the truck. Some were sitting in the back of the pickup.

The truck beeped its horn, and John moved over to the side. One of the kids stuck his head out the window.

"John Williams, right?" asked the kid.

John was surprised. None of the cool white kids had ever talked to him outside of school before. John looked at his face. It was the same white kid who had shaken his hand at the track meet.

"Yes," said John. "That's me."

Everyone in the truck started to yell. John was worried at first. He looked at them closely. They were screaming, but their faces were happy. Many of them were talking at the same time, so John couldn't understand what they were saying. Some were pointing at his medal. They were cheering for him.

John looked at them more carefully. Some of them had beer bottles in their hands. They were drunk.

"We're number one!" they yelled.

John smiled with them, though he felt a little strange.

"Get in, Williams!" said the kid who shook his hand. "We're going to celebrate!"

John paused. This was all so new and weird to him. He looked at their faces again. They seemed happy for him.

John climbed into the back of the truck. The truck sped off down the road.

"So," asked John, "where are we going?"

"We're going to celebrate!" they screamed.

The truck drove faster and faster down the streets of the border town. The faster the truck went, the more the kids screamed. John began screaming with them, this is what he had been hoping for all this time.

They drove around town for hours. The later it got, the faster they drove. Many times they turned sharply around corners. Some of the kids almost fell out. John held on to the side tightly. He wondered where they were going. He wondered what they were going to do.

As the truck turned another corner, it slowed down. On the side of the road lay a homeless Navajo. John closed his eyes. He felt embarrassed. He tried to ignore the man, but the kids started laughing at him.

The truck stopped right next to the homeless man. John started to feel nervous. The white kids hopped out of the truck.

"What are we doing?" asked John.

"Celebrating!" they screamed.

John stayed in the truck and watched. The white kids surrounded the homeless Navajo. They started pouring beer on him. They laughed as the man tried to crawl away.

"Go back to the Reservation!" screamed one of them.

One of the kids started kicking the Navajo man. Soon they were all kicking him.

John was shocked. He sat frozen in the back of the truck. He could see the face of the Navajo man. The old man didn't cry or scream. He just kept quiet. All he did was stare directly into John's eyes.

The kids continued to kick the man. The homeless Navajo's stare made John feel sick. All John could think about was his grandfather, and all the other Navajo on the Reservation. They were old memories, but they seemed new again.

John felt like he was going to throw up. He climbed out of the back of the truck. Some of the kids looked at John.

"Hey! Is he your dad?" they laughed.

John turned away from them. He started to run. He wanted to get far away from them. He wanted to run far away from everything. As he ran, tears started to run down his face. His medal bounced against his chest.

"Boy! Look at that Navajo run!" he heard the white kids cheer.

Soon John was many blocks away. He was on the far edge of town. With his back to the border town, he looked toward the Reservation. He thought he could see the glow from the few lights there.

John stopped by the side of the road. He coughed and cried. He sat down in the dirt. For the first time in his life, he questioned who he really was and where he really belonged. Was he Navajo? Was he white?

All he knew was that he, like where he sat, was somewhere between two worlds. He was somewhere in between the world of the Reservation and the border town.

He held his medal in his hands and cried.

Think About It

1. What is John's struggle in the story?

2. Why is John crying at the end?

3. If you were John's friend, what advice would you give him?

Before You Read

During the Vietnam War, many young Americans were drafted to fight. Many of those did not believe in that war. Most went to Vietnam, but there were a few who refused to fight.

Letters From the Front

Dear Mom and Dad,

As you already know, my number came up. The government is drafting me to go and fight in Vietnam.

This may be a shock to you, but I do not want to go. I do not believe in killing. I believe that it is wrong to kill another person, even if it is an enemy of this country.

I have decided to avoid the draft. I am writing you this letter to say good-bye. I cannot stay at home anymore. Because I refuse to be drafted, I will be arrested. I do not want to bring trouble into your home.

I also do not want the government to find me so I must leave. There is really nowhere I can live in this country without them looking for me. My only choice is to leave the United States. I am going north to Canada. The government cannot arrest me up there.

This means that I will probably never be able to come home again. I will no longer be able to visit you. This is what makes me really sad. It is not easy for me to do this.

I hope you can understand why I am doing this. I know that Dad served in the Army in Korea. He was drafted, too. But I cannot do.

Ever since I was small, I believed that it was wrong for people to kill other people. I do not like fighting. I have always believed there is a peaceful way to solve problems.

Do you remember the movie we saw when I was a kid? It was a Western about a man who refused to carry a gun. He solved all of his problems with his mind and his words. I wish the United States would do the same. I learned early on that there has to be another way to settle disputes besides fighting and killing. I think it takes a strong person not to fight.

Don't think I am just running away from responsibility. You may think I am a coward, but I hope you realize how much courage it is taking for me to do what I have to do now. This is the hardest decision I've ever had to make.

I am not afraid of dying. There is much more risk in what I am doing now than in going to war. Please understand why I am doing this and how hard a decision it was to make.

I really do think it is wrong to kill. My country may say it is OK, but I can't agree, I must leave my country and my family forever.

I do not mind that other people may hate me for what I am doing. I know the neighbors and other people in town will say bad things about me to you. People always hate other people because they are different. I think that is why we sometimes go to war. We fight other people just because they are different. That is how I understand it.

It is easier for some people to hate than to love. Because I will now be different, it is easier for people to hate me than to understand my choice. I understand that.

I cannot always do what other people want me to

do, especially when I know it is wrong. If people want to hate me because of who I am, or what I believe in, there is nothing I can do about it. Whether it is other people, my country, or even my family, I cannot be forced to do what I believe is wrong.

But I care about what you two think of me. I care because you are my parents and I love you. I hope you will someday be able to understand. For now I hope that you will still love me as a son. I hope you will respect my choice.

I am already on my way to Canada. You will notice that I have taken a few things with me. I have left most of my things behind, though. You can look through my room and see.

I hope to reach my destination soon. I will write to you from Canada. I hope you will find it in your heart to write me back. I will understand if you don't.

Your son,
Leonard

• • •

Dear Mom and Dad,

I am in Canada now. It was a tough trip. I had to hitchhike most of the way. I was able to find a job in a grocery store. It doesn't pay much, but it is the start of my new life. I just wanted to let you know that I am OK.

I see the war is still going on. I heard that many of the kids from our town were killed. I am sad for them and their parents. There are also many kids from the United States up here. Some are like me and they believe that killing is wrong. Others just think that the war is wrong.

This is my address now. As I wrote in my first letter, I hope you will understand why I had to leave. I hope you can forgive me and write me soon.

Your son,

Leonard

• • •

Dear Leonard,

Your father and I were very upset when we found out that you had left. We are both upset for different reasons though.

I cannot lie. I am angry with you. I am only writing this letter because your father is forcing me to. I believe that no matter what you say, what you are doing is the wrong thing.

You owe it to your country to fight when you are called to duty. Your country protects you. When your country needs you to protect it, you should be happy to go.

No one likes killing, Leonard. That's what makes us human. But there are times when we have to fight. I don't understand why you need to love everyone. I think some people don't deserve it.

Part of me is happy that you are safe. That is because I am a mother. But as a citizen of the United States, I am embarrassed that you ran away. Other mothers here in town say you are a coward. I'm afraid I have to agree with them.

The government called us here the other day looking for you. We told them that you had run away. I was so embarrassed to tell them that. The government official said you were out of their reach in Canada, but if you ever tried to come back, you could be arrested. You are now officially a criminal. You were such a good boy when you were little. I don't know where I went wrong.

I can't write anymore. I know your father thinks differently than I do. We argue about you every day and every night. What you have done is tearing our family apart. I hope you are proud of yourself.

Your father wants to write to you. I will not let him add on to my letter. I'm angry with him, too.

You should know that this will be the last time you hear from me. I'm sure your father will write to you and you can keep in touch with him. But as for me, when you said good-bye to your country, you said good-bye to me.

Mom

• • •

Dear Son,

Your mother is in the kitchen crying, writing you a letter. She won't let me share her letter to you, so I am writing to you here in the living room.

As you guessed, your decision to leave the country upset both your mother and me. But what may surprise you is that we have different reasons.

As you know, I was drafted when I was young. I had to go all the way to Korea to fight. I didn't want to have to kill anyone either, but I felt I had to go. Maybe it was just a different kind of war then. Nowadays there seem to be lots of kids doing what you did. Wars today seem more complicated than they did when I was young, or when your grandfather was young.

As you know, my father also went to war. Even though he was older than many of the kids who served, he volunteered to go. He went to Europe in the beginning of World War II. He died there. I still remember when he died. I was a teenager then and was too young to be drafted for World War II. I still miss him now. Maybe it's because of him I felt I had to go when I was drafted for service in Korea.

As a person who has actually been to war, I can tell you that I understand why you do not want to fight. Even though I served in the Army, I did not think it was as wonderful as your mother seems to think it was. I did not feel like I was a hero just because I had to kill a few people who were the "enemy."

I know that you are not a coward. Those who call you a coward have never been to war. It takes a lot of courage to stand up for what you believe in. In one way, you are doing what our country is doing. Our country is standing up for what it believes in, too. You are doing what your grandfather did. He believed he should fight. You believe you shouldn't. Both of you are very similar. I think in many ways you are the same.

I guess the only reason I am upset with you going to Canada is because you are now so far away. Your mother doesn't remember that Western movie you wrote us about, but I do. I was the one who took you to see it. I wanted you to see a peaceful movie.

Maybe I am to blame for the way you grew up. All I knew was that after I had gone to war, I wanted my son to think of peace as a better choice than war.

What makes me sad is that I may never see you again. The government called and said you are now a criminal. Your mother talks about you like you really are a criminal. I can't. I think you are really a hero, just like my dad, but in your own special way.

But I will still never be able to see you. You cannot come home anymore. I had to grow up without a dad. I wish you were still here so I could be a dad for you.

Maybe some day I can go to Canada to visit you. I would have to go alone though. As you know, your mother is not happy with you. She does not call you her son anymore.

Your mother and I argue about you sometimes. When you first left we argued a lot. I try not to now because it makes life hard when we are always fighting. Like you, I do not like to fight, even if it is just with words.

Don't be sad. Be as brave as you have been. You are still my son. I will always be your father. Even though we are thousands of miles apart, you should know that I am here for you. I will write you and I hope you will write me. I hope someday that we can meet again in person. That would be the happiest day for me.

Write soon, and wear a warm coat.

Love,

Dad

Think About It

1. Why is Leonard's mother so angry at him?

2. Why does Leonard's father compare Leonard to his father?

3. This story presents a very complicated issue. Which person do you agree with the most? Why?

Before You Read

Sometimes you feel pressured to do something just because your friends say it's OK. In this story, a teenager struggles to do the right thing in a difficult situation.

Food for Thought

"I'm hungry," said Carmen's best friend Julie. "Let's stop by Mrs. Fernandez's store."

They always stopped in Mrs. Fernandez's store on the way home from school. Carmen and her friends had been going there for years.

Mrs. Fernandez was a nice old woman. She was always friendly to the girls, especially Carmen. She would always give them extras when they bought candy in her store. She would make them very large sandwiches even when they ordered small ones. Sometimes she gave them free snacks even when they didn't ask for them.

Carmen, Julie, and the others went inside the store. Julie and the others went up and down the aisles. Even though Carmen wasn't going to buy anything, she stopped to talk with Mrs. Fernandez. She liked talking with her.

After a few minutes Julie grabbed Carmen by the shoulder.

"Come on," said Julie. "We're leaving."

"Aren't you going to buy anything?" asked Carmen.

"Not today," said Julie.

"See you tomorrow, girls," waved Mrs. Fernandez, as they left.

As they walked down the street, the girls stopped and started laughing. Carmen didn't understand why.

"Why are you all laughing?" asked Carmen.

"Look what we got!" said Julie. The girls pulled candy bars and other snacks out of their pockets.

"I thought you didn't buy anything," said Carmen.

"We didn't," laughed Julie. "We stole this stuff."

Carmen was shocked. She couldn't understand why they had stolen things from nice old Mrs. Fernandez.

"Why did you do that?" asked Carmen.

"Because we wanted to," said Julie. "It's fun."

Carmen didn't know what to say.

"You shouldn't steal," said Carmen.

"Why not?"

"Because it's wrong."

The girls laughed and stuck their tongues out at Carmen.

"We do it all the time," said Julie. "It's the cool thing to do."

Carmen didn't know what to say. What was wrong with Julie?

"I think you shouldn't do that," said Carmen.

"Oh, come on Carmen," laughed Julie. "How old are you?"

"I'm as old as you are, Julie."

"Maybe, but you're acting like a baby," said Julie. "Everyone steals. It's just candy. Mrs. Fernandez won't miss it. She gives us this stuff for free anyway."

"I don't know," said Carmen. "I still think stealing is wrong. Mrs. Fernandez is nice enough to give food to us for free. I don't think you should just take it from her."

"Mrs. Fernandez is too old to notice. She won't even know it's missing."

"I still think it's a bad thing to do," said Carmen.

"Look," said Julie. "Now that we're in junior high, we have to start acting like we're older."

"So? Being older doesn't mean stealing," said Carmen.

"Sometimes it does," said Julie. "My mom even does it."

"Really?"

"Yeah. She steals pens and stuff from her office all the time."

"I don't want to be a criminal," said Carmen.

"A criminal?" laughed Julie. "We're not stealing TVs or cars. We're only stealing little things. It's fun and it's cool to get away with stealing little things."

"I don't know," said Carmen.

"Have you ever tried it?" one girl asked.

"No!" said Carmen.

"You should. I think you should try it at least once," said Julie. "Everyone needs a little danger. A little danger helps you grow up faster."

Carmen shook her head. She couldn't believe this was her friend talking. She looked at all the other girls. They were already eating their food.

"You're not going to tell on us, are you?" asked Julie.

Carmen didn't know what to say. All the girls stopped munching. They were looking at her.

"No, I guess I won't," said Carmen.

"Good," said Julie. "You're part of our club now."

"What club?" asked Carmen.

"The Five Finger Discount Club," the girls said.

"What kind of club is that?" asked Carmen.

"It's a cool club for people like us who like a little danger."

"What kind of danger?"

"Shoplifting," said Julie. She held up her hand and counted her fingers. "These five fingers can get you things for free."

"They can also get you into trouble," said Carmen.

"That's the fun part," said Julie.

"I don't know if I want to be part of your club then," said Carmen.

"Come on, Carmen," said Julie. "Live a little. If you aren't part of our club, you can't hang out with us."

Carmen looked around her. All the girls were looking at her. She felt confused. She couldn't believe what they were doing. She had always been friends with them. Why did they have to go and make up a dumb club like that?

"Could I still be part of the club," asked Carmen, "if I don't steal?" She didn't want to lose her friends. They were the only friends she had.

Julie and the girls laughed. "It's not as easy as that," said Julie. "If you want to be one of us you have to steal, at least once."

"I'll think about it," said Carmen.

For the next few weeks that's all Carmen could think about. Every time they stopped by Mrs. Fernandez's store, Carmen felt strange.

Every day the girls stole something. Carmen saw them, but she tried to ignore it. But every day they would tease her and try to make Carmen join in.

One day Julie said, "Carmen. You're going to have to steal at least once if you want to hang out with us now."

Carmen looked at her.

"I'll think about it," said Carmen.

"You'd better," said Julie. "Some of the other girls don't feel comfortable with you not stealing. They're afraid you're going to tell on us."

"I won't tell," said Carmen.

"I know that, but the others aren't sure anymore. They feel they can't trust you if you haven't stolen anything. You've got to do it at least once."

Carmen looked down at her feet. She said nothing.

"Look," said Julie, "it's really easy. Just take a small candy bar. You only have to do it once, then you'll be OK."

"Just once?" asked Carmen.

"Sure. We'll do it tomorrow after school," said Julie, patting Carmen on the back. "If you don't do it by the end of this week, you can't be one of us."

The next day, Carmen stood in Mrs. Fernandez's store with a candy bar that she had put in her pocket. Julie had told her how to steal. Julie was right, it was easy enough. Carmen was wearing her big winter coat. It had big pockets. Now all she had to do was walk out the door and hope nobody stopped her.

"Why am I doing this?" she thought.

As Carmen got closer to the door she stopped. Her heart was beating fast. She felt like everyone was watching her. She felt that everyone knew what she was about to do.

"Why am I doing this?" Carmen asked herself again.

Carmen decided to stop and think about it some more. She walked to the side of the store, away from Mrs. Fernandez's register and away from the door.

From where she stood she could see out the store window. Her friends were waiting for her to come out with the stolen candy bar. Julie glared at her through the glass.

Carmen nodded back. But she still stayed in the store. She walked up and down the side of the store thinking to herself.

"This is wrong," she thought. "I can't do this to Mrs. Fernandez."

"What are you doing?" Carmen heard from behind her. It startled her. She turned around. It was only Julie.

"What are you waiting for? We're all waiting for you."

"I don't know if I can do it," whispered Carmen.

"Of course you can," whispered Julie.

"I still think it's wrong."

"Don't be chicken," said Julie. "Don't let me down."

Carmen closed her eyes. She tried to think. She felt confused.

"Did you pick up anything?" asked Julie.

Carmen nodded and patted her coat pocket.

"Good," said Julie. "Now just come out with me."

"I'm scared," said Carmen.

"That's part of the fun," said Julie.

"It doesn't seem like fun to me," Carmen whispered.

"You'll think it's fun after you do it," said Julie.

"I just can't do it," said Carmen.

Julie shook her head. She reached into Carmen's pocket and pulled out the candy bar.

"Good choice," said Julie, looking at the candy bar. "I think I'll take this one for myself."

Carmen watched Julie put it into her pocket.

"I'll give you another five minutes," warned Julie. "If you don't have anything by then, we're leaving without you."

"But ...," started Carmen.

"No 'buts,'" said Julie. "Five minutes."

Carmen watched Julie turn around and head for the door. She was almost there when Julie bumped into Mrs. Fernandez.

"Hi, Julie," said Mrs. Fernandez.

Julie ran out the door without saying hello.

"Maybe she didn't hear me," said Mrs. Fernandez. "You girls always seem to be in a rush lately."

Carmen nodded nervously.

"Maybe it's because of all that candy you kids eat," said Mrs. Fernandez.

Carmen gasped. Did Mrs. Fernandez know what had been going on? She must know. The girls had practically stolen everything in her store in the last few weeks. Surely she had noticed all that food had gone.

But did she know?

"Carmen?" asked Mrs. Fernandez. "Are you OK?"

Carmen nodded, but she was really feeling sick.

"I think you should come and sit down in the back," said Mrs. Fernandez.

Carmen walked back with Mrs. Fernandez. Mrs. Fernandez opened the door to the back room. She brought Carmen into a small comfortable room, with a nice soft chair.

"I sometimes have to sit back here when I get tired," said Mrs. Fernandez. "Running a store all by yourself can be tough, especially when you're as old as I am."

Carmen sat down. She didn't know what to say. Did Mrs. Fernandez know what was going on?

"I like you girls," said Mrs. Fernandez. "You remind me of when I was young."

Mrs. Fernandez smiled at Carmen. Carmen smiled too, nervously.

"You girls are like my own children," said Mrs. Fernandez. "Maybe that's why I like to spoil all of you."

"You're too kind," said Carmen.

"I know," said Mrs. Fernandez. "But if it means a candy bar or two every now and then, I don't mind."

Carmen looked at Mrs. Fernandez. She knew. She had to know. Though she was old, she wasn't dumb. But Carmen wasn't sure. Carmen couldn't stand her being so nice anymore.

Carmen reached into her pocket. She pulled out some money and gave it to Mrs. Fernandez.

"Carmen," said Mrs. Fernandez. "What's this for?"

"For the candy."

"Oh," said Mrs. Fernandez. "Did you want to buy some? I'll give it to you for free. It's nice to have someone to talk to."

"But …," said Carmen.

"No 'buts.' You're my friend, Carmen. You're like a daughter to me. I think I can afford to give you candy."

Before Carmen could say anything, Mrs. Fernandez got up. She walked back out into the store. Carmen followed her.

Mrs. Fernandez went over to where the candy bars were. She grabbed more than one. She put them in a bag and gave them to Carmen.

"Here," said Mrs. Fernandez, "here's some for you and your nice friends."

Carmen felt embarrassed.

"Can I give you some money?" she asked.

"Oh no!" said Mrs. Fernandez. "You girls are like my daughters. I want you to have it."

"Thank you," said Carmen. She reached for the bag. Mrs. Fernandez held onto it first.

"You just have to promise me one thing, Carmen," said Mrs. Fernandez.

"Oh no," thought Carmen. "She knows."

"Promise me that you will stop by and chat for a little longer," said Mrs. Fernandez.

"OK," said Carmen. Mrs. Fernandez gave her the bag of candy.

Carmen took the bag. She stuffed it into her coat pocket. As she walked toward the door, she turned and looked at the old woman. She smiled and went outside.

Julie and the girls ran up to her.

"It's about time!" said Julie. "Where's the candy?"

"I don't have it," said Carmen.

"What?" said Julie. "You spent all that time in there and didn't steal a thing?"

"No," said Carmen.

All the girls rolled their eyes. They started to walk away from Carmen. Carmen watched them turn their backs on her. She didn't feel as bad as she thought she would.

"Well, you know this means you can't be part of our club," warned Julie. "That means we can't hang out together."

"I know," said Carmen.

Julie ran off to catch up with the rest of the girls. Carmen stood alone by the store and watched them go.

Carmen pulled the bag of candy out of her coat pocket. She looked at it. She then turned and looked at the store. She opened the door and went back in to talk with her friend, Mrs. Fernandez.

Think About It

1. Why does Carmen have a hard time shoplifting?

2. Do you think that Mrs. Fernandez knew that the girls were stealing? Why or why not?

3. What advice would you give Julie? What advice would you give Mrs. Fernandez?

Before You Read
Dolores Huerta has fought all her life for the rights of farm workers. Although she is old now, she still struggles to make sure workers are treated fairly.

Dolores Huerta: Fighting for the Right

Dolores Huerta came from a family that always tried to help people. Like her parents, she eventually found her own way of helping those who needed it the most.

Her father, who had been a miner and field worker in New Mexico, had worked to protect the rights of poor workers. He had worked in the state government and had served as a state assemblyman.

Dolores's mother had owned and run a seventy-room hotel. Many poor farmer families lived there. Because they were poor, Dolores's mother let them live there for free.

So from an early age, Dolores Huerta understood that people needed help. She saw how the farm workers in her mother's hotel struggled to make a living. She saw how difficult it was for them to get by.

After college, Dolores Huerta first tried working as a teacher. She taught in a grammar school where many farm workers' children went. Many poor children were in her classes. Many children came to class without shoes. Many were always hungry.

Dolores felt sad for them. She decided to do something to help the children.

Dolores left her job as a teacher. She started working to help the poor farm workers and their families. She believed that she could help them more that way than as a teacher.

Farm workers in California had a hard life. They were paid little money for the hard work that they did. Many of the farm owners treated their workers very badly. Often the workers were treated badly because they weren't white.

The owners would make their workers work long hours. Sometimes they worked in places that were very dangerous.

Many workers were poor. They were often abused. Many of them were Hispanic. They had to struggle with racism and prejudice. They were treated unfairly, not just by their bosses, but by their government.

The police were known to treat them cruelly. The needs and rights of the farm workers seemed unimportant. They were treated like second-class citizens. They had no voice or person to help them.

Dolores decided to be that voice.

In 1955, Dolores started her new life helping people. She joined the Community Service Organization. It was one of the largest Hispanic civil rights movements in the country. The group worked hard to protect the rights of Hispanic workers. It protected them from the abuse of racist bosses and local governments. The group worked hard to end the abuse workers found in their jobs and in their lives.

Dolores worked hard to stop police brutality. She helped workers to have a voice in their government. She registered many of them to vote. She helped the workers get the public help they deserved. She helped create new laws. The laws protected workers who were hurt while at their jobs.

In 1962, with César Chávez, Dolores founded the National Farm Workers Association. It started out as a small union. Only three years later, the union had more than 1,200 member-families. That same year, their union joined a large strike against the Central Valley grape producers.

The grape growers in California were treating their workers badly. They paid their workers very little. They forced the grape pickers to work in unsafe conditions.

To protect the grapes against insects, the grapes were sprayed with dangerous chemicals. But the chemicals were also poisonous to people as well as to insects. Many workers became sick just from picking the grapes.

Dolores Huerta's group joined other workers' unions to increase their power as a group. The larger the union, the more people would be forced to listen to their cause. Together the unions worked to stop the grape growers. They organized a massive strike. Workers walked off their jobs in protest. They wanted the owners to change the way they were treating them. They wanted the grape growers to stop using the poisonous chemicals. The strike was known as the Delano Grape Strike.

As a union leader, Dolores met with the growers many times. Through hard work and tough negotiations, she was able to create better contracts for the workers. She helped write the union's first contract with the grape growers.

But the grape growers were rich and powerful. They did everything they could to try and stop Dolores and the union. Sometimes they sent men to bully the workers who were on strike. Many times they tried to have the government arrest the strikers. Dolores was arrested many times, just for fighting for the workers' rights.

The growers' power did not stop Dolores Huerta. She continued to organize more strikes. She continued to get workers to vote. They were able to elect people into the government who could help them. She spoke to newspapers and others about the dangerous chemicals the grape growers were using.

She warned people across the country. She made people realize that the poisons were hurting the grape pickers. She also let them know that the chemicals could poison people who ate the grapes. She encouraged many people to stop buying California grapes.

The farm workers' cause was always the most important for Dolores Huerta, even in her personal life. She continued to fight even when she was pregnant. Even after having eleven children, Dolores would not stop. She changed diapers and took care of her babies during meetings with the grape owners.

For more than twenty years, Dolores Huerta has continued to fight for workers' rights. She has become a very important political figure. Many famous political people were able to win elections because of her support. Senator Robert Kennedy thanked Dolores for his success in the 1968 California primary elections. She even served as one of the co-chairs for California at the 1972 Democratic Convention.

Dolores Huerta continues to fight for the fair treatment of workers today. Even as a grandmother of ten children, she continues to work hard for her union.

In 1988, Dolores Huerta was still on the front lines of the battle for workers' rights. In San Francisco, she handed out papers about the union's grape boycott. She did this near where then Vice-President Bush was speaking. Even though she was an old woman, the police arrested her. They knocked her down with clubs. She needed emergency surgery for a ruptured spleen and three broken ribs.

But even with all the danger, the fight for the workers is still important to Dolores Huerta. Today she still travels across the country. She tells people about the dangers of poisoned California grapes and the needs of the workers who pick them.

Think About It

1. One of the many things Dolores Huerta did for farm workers was to get them to register to vote. Why was that important?

2. Why did farm workers go on strike against the California grape growers?

3. Do you think that not buying grapes could change the way workers are treated?

Sometimes we can be pushed too far. When that happens, we might do something that we would not normally do.

What Johnny Did

J.N. Fox

They asked why
Johnny did the thing he did.

His friend said, " I don't know,"
but remembered the morning
when the big kid beat him.

A teacher said, "I don't know,"
but remembered the lunch time
when the big kid teased him.

The school guard said, "I don't know,"
but remembered the afternoon
when the big kid chased him.

His mother cried, "I don't know,"
but remembered the nights
when the big kid filled his dreams.

They asked why
Johnny did the thing he did.

Think About It

1. What do you think Johnny did?

2. Are there any clues in the poem that might suggest what he did?

3. If Johnny came to you for advice, what would tell him?

Before You Read

Homelessness is a big problem in this country. Every day homeless people struggle to survive. Here is a man who speaks out about what it is like to be homeless.

Homeless: A Personal Story

I didn't ask to be homeless. Nobody asks to live the way I do. Sometimes it's just the way things happen. Sometimes life doesn't happen the way you think it will. Sometimes things happen the way you never thought they would.

Because I live on the streets, many people forget that I'm a regular person. They forget that I'm a living, breathing human being, just like everyone else.

When people look at me, all they can see is a bum. All they see is a guy who has no place to go. People think I'm an animal or something. I can tell that by the way they stare at me. I can tell that even more by the way they ignore me.

Many people can't see past the fact that I have to live on the streets. Many people just don't want to see the truth.

I didn't always live like this. I once had a home. I even had a family. Believe it or not, I am not that much different from you or anybody else. Don't forget that I was once like you.

What happened to me could happen to any one of you.

I had a mom and dad, just like everybody else. I was once somebody's son. I still am. You can't avoid that in this world.

My family was the same as most of yours. We just had a bit more bad luck than other families.

Believe it or not, we weren't a poor family. We had enough money to get by. We weren't rich, but we were OK. We got by. We had a house. We even had a car. We just had a little bad luck, that's all.

My father was a good man. He had a paying job. He used to work in a factory. My mom worked, too. I forget what she did. It was a long time ago. Whatever she did, she had to work a lot like my dad did. No one would ever call him lazy.

We were all just like normal people at one point. We had a place to live. I went to school. Mom and Dad went to work every day. There's nothing so weird about that. We could have been your neighbors. We could have even been you. Like I said, sometimes things just happen.

One day my dad lost his job. He was laid off. These things happen a lot nowadays. My mom still had her job, so things weren't that bad at first.

But as I said, we weren't rich. We had debts to pay. I was only a kid then, so I really didn't understand it all. All I remember is that at some point, my mom and dad started worrying a lot. Sometimes they would yell at each other.

I know Mom was tired of working so hard. I don't blame her. Dad wasn't able to find a new job. I remember my mom yelling at him to try. He said he was, but Mom said he wasn't. All I could see was that every day, when I got home from school, Dad would still be hangin' around the house.

I remember telling my folks that I would try to get a job. I wasn't dumb. I knew we needed the money. I wanted to help.

But my folks didn't want me to. I think they were too proud. They said I should stay in school while I could. I think they always thought things would turn out better. As you probably can guess, they didn't. They got worse.

One day I came home from school. My folks were yelling again. For whatever reason, we had run out of money. Even though Mom was working hard enough, it still wasn't enough to get by.

At first things weren't that bad. We sold a few things here and there. We sold our TV and other stuff we didn't really need. We still ate OK. We still had a roof over our heads.

But soon, we were low on money again. I remember the electric company turned the power off. We had to use candles for light. I remember I hated it because I could never see well enough to read and do my homework.

I think we were a little lucky because it was still summer at that point. But it was hot having all those candles lit, and I hated the heat. But I remember worrying about what we would have to do when it got cold. Even though it was hot then, I knew candles couldn't heat the house.

Well, one day I came back from school and I saw Mom and Dad moving what stuff we had left into the car. I didn't know what was going on. Were we moving? Where are we going?

I asked my dad what was happening. He said we had lost the house. I remember joking that he should have kept his eyes on it. Nobody laughed. It was a dumb thing to have said, really. I shut up and helped finish packing the car.

I asked about what we were going to do. My folks said they didn't know. I think that was the first time I realized that things weren't going to be OK. Mom and Dad had always had a plan.

You may have guessed it, but we had to start living in the car. Dad drove off to another part of town. We parked in a quiet place. It was a bit weird at first. I missed my bed. We all had to sleep sitting up in the seats. I kind of miss that now, really.

My mom still had her job, which was really strange. I don't think she told the people she worked for what was really going on. She would get dressed up and go to work like nothing had happened.

Well, for a while we did have some money coming in, but it was really only enough for us to eat. We weren't eating like kings, but we weren't starving either.

Many of you must wonder what it's like living out of a car. I can tell you, it's not fun. You do all you can to try and stay outside. You walk around a lot. You have to take showers in public bathrooms.

When Mom would go off to work, Dad and I would walk around looking for a job for him. Nobody seemed to want to hire a guy who lived out of his car. I think they thought Dad must have been too weird to work. It was tough watching all those people giving him strange looks.

Sometimes we would just hang around the car. Because we had all of our stuff in there, we had to keep guarding it. Guys were always trying to break in and get our stuff.

One guy managed to break our window. He stole only a few things. But we didn't have much anyway. All I remember was being angry. It was harder to stay warm in a car when you had a broken window. It was winter. Sometimes the snow would fall right into the car.

At that point things got worse. My dad got pretty sick. I'm sure if he hadn't, we might have been able to do better. Who knows? At that point, he had just been able to find a job. He had stopped telling employers that we were living in our car.

But because he was now sick, he had to miss work. Whoever had given him the chance gave up on Dad pretty quickly. Dad couldn't help being sick. He lived in an open car. But the guy who hired him quickly fired him. Just as nobody wants to hire a guy who lives in his car, nobody wants to pay for a worker who is always sick. Poor Dad never got better.

At that point, I spent most of my time walking around. I wasn't in school anymore, so I had lots of time on my hands. I think I was starting to get embarrassed at what had happened to us. Dad was sick, and Mom was getting more and more upset with everything. I don't know why, but I just didn't like hanging around them. I did everything I could to get away.

I would go to the library and read. In fact, I read lots of books there. I think I've read more books than many of you have. I would stay in that warm library all day, just to avoid going back to the car. Sometimes if I was lucky, I could hide in the library when they closed for the night. I would sleep there.

It got to the point where I would stay away for days. I had been able to figure out a way to live in the library without anyone noticing. I would only go to the car once in a while to change my clothes.

I would check on my dad, too. He seemed to be getting worse. I would try to take care of him, but he always seemed cold. Maybe I could have tried harder, but I was just a dumb kid then. Who knows what I could have done to help the poor guy out? Part of me is still angry with how I acted. I wish I knew then what I know now. I might have made a difference.

All I knew was that it was warmer in the library. I had a good thing going there. I think I did try to get my dad to go there with me, but he was too sick to walk that far. He said it was better that I go and stay warm while I could.

Maybe I was dumb to do so, but I listened to him. I left him and went back to the library.

After a week of hiding out in the library some more, I went home. (I know it was just a car, but what else should I call it?) When I got there I found it empty. Everything was gone. Even my dad.

My guess is that he finally got so sick that Mom took him to a hospital. I don't know for sure, really. I'd like to believe that he got some medical attention. I think he might have died there. I'd like to believe that. I'd like to think that he died in a warm place, and not on the street, or in that car.

My guess, or really my hope, is that Mom must have taken him somewhere. Again I don't know, really. All I knew was that I had lost them. I had been spending so much time living in that library, they must have thought I'd run away.

At that point, I made an effort to stay near the front of library. I used to stay way in the back. It was easier to hang out there and hide if people didn't see you around so much. But now I was hanging around the front. That was a mistake. I thought I had to hang out in a place where I could be found.

I was sure that my dad must have told Mom where I was sleeping. I was sure she would come for me. But she never did. I waited in the front, just in case. I wanted to make it easier for her. I'd like to believe they didn't give up on me, but who knows? Maybe it was easier for them to try and get along without me. For all I know, my dad is still alive. For all I know, he and my mom are OK now. But I can only guess.

At that point I'd been hanging around the library too much. The people who worked there and some of the guards must have guessed what I was doing. I mean, after all, I was always where they could see me.

It had become more obvious after Mom and Dad disappeared. I was hanging around the front every day, all day. I should have hidden in the back, but I was still waiting for Mom to come and find me.

That was my mistake. They finally kicked me out of the library. I didn't mind at that point, really. I think I must've read all their books by then.

I guess what bothers me the most is that they didn't care. They didn't seem to figure out that I had no other place to live. Even if they did figure it out, they didn't do anything to help me. I didn't ask them to help, so it wasn't all their fault. But still, they seemed more eager to get me out than to help me out.

I think that's what annoys me the most. People always seem to want to help other people when they're down and out. But you have to be down and out for a while before you get their attention. By then you don't want it.

That's when I started living on the streets. I've been on my own now for ten years. You're probably wondering how I lasted so long on my own. I'll tell you that there are a lot of ways. I hope you don't have to learn to survive on the streets.

I just keep moving. That's what I do. I've been doing it for so long now, I don't know how to sit still. I've spent time in shelters. I eat in free kitchens here and there. I get clothes where and how I can. When it's warm enough, I just sleep on the streets.

I've met lots of people like me out on the streets. I learned from them, really. I didn't realize it at first, but they sort of became my new family.

Like a family, we do what we can to help each other out. If somebody finds an abandoned house to sleep in, we all sleep there. When someone has a bit of good luck, we try and share it. Too bad there's not a lot of good luck to go around. Maybe that way we could all get along a little better.

I see that you're looking at me funny. Don't worry, I'm used to it by now. You're probably wondering if I'm telling you the truth. Believe me, the truth is the only thing I have. My story is the only thing I have that I know is mine for sure.

You may be thinking, Why doesn't he just get a job? He can read. Well, it sounds easier than it really is. People take one look at me and decide not to give me a chance. Living on the streets doesn't make you pretty. Sure, I've had a few small jobs here and there, moving and carrying heavy things. But nobody seems to want to hire a guy, no matter how smart he seems, when he's lived on the streets.

You may also be wondering how old I am now. What, can't you tell? If you can't tell, I won't tell you.

I'll just say this. People think I'm a lot older than I really am. I'm still a young person, really. I just look old. I've been through a lot.

It's good to look older when you live on the streets. Not too old—then people kick you around. Just old enough so that people don't bother you.

When they think you're a kid, lots of creeps try and bother you. Sometimes they want to take advantage of you. Sometimes they're just nice people trying to help you out. Someone once, when I was younger, tried to help me. She must have been a social worker or something. She was always bugging me and the other kids on the street.

I don't know why I hated it, but I always tried to get away from her as fast as I could. I would tell her that I still had my parents, and that we still had a house.

Of course she didn't believe me. She wasn't stupid. She tried as hard as she could to track me down. She wanted to put me up somewhere with another family. I just couldn't handle that. Maybe I was too proud. Like I said, I was just a dumb kid then. I just kept lying to her and moving around.

In time, she gave up on me. Part of me is a little sad that she did. Maybe if I had to do it again, I might have taken her up on her offer.

But as you can tell, I didn't, and I'm too old for that now. Would you adopt me?

I don't know why I lied to that lady. I guess part of me thought that if I did try and live with another family, I would be betraying my parents. I had a family, I thought. I didn't know where they were, but I had one. I didn't need other people trying to find me a new one.

All that was years ago, when I thought I could find my mom. That was some time ago. Maybe I should try to find them. I don't know if I want to try. Who knows what I'll find out?

Well, that's my story so far. I'm not going to bore you with any more details. Like I said, this is the only story I have. It's the only thing I have. It's what makes me, me.

If anything, you should know this. There are lots of us out here on the streets. Sure, we all have sad stories to tell, but you should remember that these aren't made-up stories.

They are real, because we are real people. We have real feelings. We have real hopes. We have real dreams.

Don't treat us like animals just because of the way we live. At least we're alive. I know some of you out there wish we weren't alive. There are some of us who think that way, too.

Many of us have been out here for so long we don't know any other way to live. That's the saddest thing. Sure we all want to get off the streets. Like I said, nobody wants to live like we do. But after a while it seems like we can't live any other way. I don't know if I could live in a house anymore. Maybe I have become kind of an animal. Just don't think of me that way.

I've known many people who've just given up. Maybe that's what I have done, at least for now. Who knows what may happen? Right now I can only think about where I'm going to sleep tonight. I can only think about where I can get some food. I can only think about staying safe and warm.

But I do know that some people have been able to get off the streets. I assume they have. I don't see them around. I just hope they're doing better. Part of me has to believe that they're doing better. Now more than ever, I see whole families, starting off the way I once did. I just hope they have better luck than I did. No one should be forced to live this way.

Sad? Yeah I know. It's all sad.

I've said enough for now. You're probably bored. Let me just finish off with this. For all of us who have given up, there are plenty more of us who haven't. When we ask for your help, try and give it to us. Don't go judging and forcing things on us when we don't ask for your help. That's annoying. But don't ignore us when we do ask. It takes a lot to ask someone else for help.

Don't look through us as if we don't exist. We do. I know it might make you feel uneasy, but that's the way life is. You can't avoid reality. Maybe you have that luxury. Many of us don't.

So give us a chance when we ask for one, just like you would anybody else. Many of us can still work. Many of us still have our minds. Like me, many of us are smart and can work. We just had some bad luck, that's all.

All we need is a break. Not a handout, but a chance. I don't like pity. Pity is when you help someone you have given up on. A chance is when you help someone you still believe can do better.

With the right opportunity we could not only make ourselves better, but our country, and even our world. Who knows?

Think About It

1. This story is best read out loud. Have someone read it out loud. How does the story seem different when you hear it?

2. The person speaking in this story says he didn't want to live with a new family. Why?

3. Name one thing that would have made this person's life easier. Explain your choice.

Many Chinese people came to the United States hoping for a better life. But many of them were not welcome. Here is the story of how one Chinese family struggled to come to America.

An Angel on Angel Island

Dearest Granddaughter,

I just received your mother's letter today. I was so happy to hear that you are coming West. You do not know how glad I am to hear that you will be visiting me in San Francisco.

During your first visit, I want to show you many things. I'm sure your mother will want to come along with us. It has been a long time since she was here.

Of course, we will go to all the places the tourists always visit, here in the Bay Area. We will ride the cable cars downtown. We will see the Golden Gate Bridge. Of course, you will see Chinatown. Our family has lived in Chinatown ever since we came to this country years ago.

I think the first thing you will notice when you visit me is that there are many more Chinese American people here than where you live in the East. That is easy to understand, if you know your history. Many Chinese who came to this country first landed in San Francisco. Many of us decided to stay here once we arrived in this country.

Your mother tells me that you are just starting to study U.S. history in school. She tells me that you are also becoming interested in our own family history. That is wonderful. It is important that you know the story of how your family came to this country. You will find out that our story is somewhat different from the ones some of your classmates may have.

For that special reason, when you arrive here, we will be taking a boat trip over to Angel Island. Angel Island has a nice name, doesn't it? Many parts of the island are beautiful. I heard that Native Americans used to live there. There is a park on the island now, with many walking trails. It looked quite different when I first saw it. Has your mother told you about Angel Island? It is an important place in our family's history.

Angel Island is important to us because it was the place where your great-grandmother arrived when she first came to this country from China. I was with her, too, many years ago. I was just a little girl then. I was younger than you are now.

Angel Island has been called the Ellis Island of the West. Your mother tells me that you also have studied Ellis Island. As you know, Ellis Island was the place where all the immigrants from Europe landed when they came to New York. Angel Island was the place where many people from Asia, mostly Chinese, landed when they first came to San Francisco.

At the immigration station on Angel, people were sorted into different groups by officials. Some were allowed to enter the United States. Others were held there and sent back to Asia.

Many Chinese had been coming to the United States for years before my mother and I did. So many Chinese had come over that some Americans did not want any more of us in the country. There was even a law that was made to keep out as many Chinese as possible. The law said that only merchants and those Chinese who had family already living here could enter the United States. They were trying to keep out the Chinese who had come to work. At that point, many Americans did not want poor Chinese people to come here and take away from American workers.

When we arrived on Angel Island, the station was filled with hundreds of other Chinese. You could tell that many of them were poor and were coming to the United States to work.

The law would prevent those people from entering the country. But many of them had hopes of lying and tricking the immigration officials on Angel Island. Because of them, the immigration people made it hard for everyone else coming in. They asked many questions and they checked all of our papers.

I can understand why they did what they did. So many people were lying. But I still resent the way they treated many of us. When my mother first arrived, many of the white officials were rude to us. They treated us like animals more than people. I got the feeling that they just didn't like the Chinese. I didn't understand why they would treat us this way.

We had a lawful reason for coming to America. My mother had family who lived here already. We weren't sure where they were, but your great-grandmother was a dreamer. She believed she could find them. She really wanted to live in America. Even in China, we had heard what a wonderful country this was. We wanted to have a better life.

When we arrived, we went through many tests on Angel Island. They asked us where we were from and where we were going. They looked through our bags. They even had doctors look at us. My mother was a shy woman and was very embarrassed by the inspections. She was not comfortable talking to strangers. She was not confident like American women are today.

The doctors were looking for diseases. They looked at our teeth to see if we had a disease called liver fluke. We had heard about how strict the Angel Island people were about diseases from China. My mother made sure we were healthy before we left. She made sure we stayed healthy on the boat trip as well.

There were many Chinese with us on the island. I remember the doctor turning many of them away. But they didn't find anything wrong with us. I think the immigration doctor wanted to, but he didn't. Mother had been smart to keep us healthy.

We had been lucky at that point. I was sure that we would soon be allowed to come into America. But then our luck changed. One of the last men to inspect us asked us many questions. He looked like the kind of man who did not trust people. He looked like he hated the Chinese people.

When we got to him, he started asking my mother strange questions. First he asked us why we had left China. He asked us again why we were coming to the United States. When my mother said that we had family in the country, he started asking even more questions.

He asked my mother for their names. He asked for their birthdays. He asked these questions over and over again. I think he was trying to see if mother was lying. Liars don't always remember the right answers to questions. They sometimes change their answers. He listened very carefully to her answers. He wrote everything she said in a big notebook.

Mother was not lying, though, and all of her answers were the same. But the immigration man asked mother where our family lived. My mother was an honest person, so she said she didn't know. This seemed to make the man happy. He grabbed mother's papers and stamped them. He had turned her down. She would not be allowed to enter the country. At first mother didn't understand. We had been cleared by the many officers before. She didn't expect to be turned down now. But when she tried to walk past him, the man stopped her. He started yelling at her. He seemed happy when he made Mother cry. He told her she had to go back to China.

Mother cried and cried. She had never expected to be turned away. We had heard horror stories in China from people who had been sent back. They had called the immigration people white devils and had sworn revenge for the bad things that had happened to them. They never told how bad it was though. Maybe they were trying not to scare us too much. But now that mother had been turned away, we would soon find out what those horrors were.

Mother and I were taken with many other Chinese to another part of the station. We were moved into the barracks. The barracks were wooden buildings that had holding cells like prisons. The Chinese who had not passed the tests were kept there. They would then be sent home to China.

The women had separate barracks from the men. The immigration people forced mother and me into a large room. Even though it was large, it was packed with other Chinese women. There must have been more than thirty people crammed into that space.

Mother held onto my hand as we tried to make our

way into the room. I remember how dirty it was in there. The air was stale and damp. It smelled like rotten things.

Mother and I were able to find a place near the wall. I noticed there were lots of things carved and written on the walls. I asked my mother to read them for me. When she did she started to cry. I cried, too. I wasn't sure why I was crying.

Poems and other graffiti were written on the walls. Some were crude, but many were beautiful. They had been written by other Chinese women who had been forced to stay in the cell. Some told the story of women who were hopeful that they would get out. Others were angry at being treated so badly. But most of them were sad. They had been written by the women who knew they were going to be sent back to China. They wrote about their sadness and shame in being turned away from the United States.

One of the women in the cell heard my mother reading the poems on the wall. She laughed at us. That woman was a tough person. I suppose she had to be. Mother started talking to her. It turned out that she had been on Angel Island, in that smelly crowded cell, for three months.

My mother asked her why she had been there so long. Some people get out in less than two weeks, the woman said. But some people have been there as long as two years. Some people never leave, she said. I started to cry.

At this point, I remember my mother covering my ears. I later understood what the woman had meant. Some women were so ashamed about being turned away from America that they had hung themselves. They would rather die on Angel Island, close to

America, than endure the shame of returning to China.

Mother and I stayed in the crowded cell for two days. I will never forget how filthy it was. We were treated like animals, not like people. There wasn't even a place to go to the bathroom. Some people just used the floor. To my mother, whose house was always clean, it was terrible.

When they served us meals, the food was terrible. We weren't used to American food then, which was all they served us. We wondered if all American food was so bad. But I know now that the food we had to eat was just bad. We were prisoners and the food they fed us wasn't good enough to feed pigs.

I remember that mother and I were able to get close to the window one day. It was always crowded with people. Some were looking out. Others were just trying to breathe some fresh air. When we got our chance at the window, mother would hold me up to see. From where we were, we could see the ferry going back and forth between Angel Island and the mainland. To the west we saw San Francisco. We could see Oakland as well. We didn't know what these places were, really. All we knew was that these places were America. We were so close. Would we ever get there?

At that point, we began to worry about what was going to happen to us. There was talk in the barracks that some would get another chance to try and get into America. My mother started talking to other women. She met one woman who seemed sure she would get in. She had relatives right in San Francisco who were coming to claim her. Because the laws only allowed Chinese who could prove they had family in America, she was sure she would get in.

My mother made a deal with her. I forget how she convinced the woman. I think she was just kind and nice enough to want to help us. Maybe she bribed her. In any case, my mother made the woman promise that she would take me into America with her. She wanted the woman to pretend I was her daughter.

I was surprised. I remember crying. I thought Mother didn't love me anymore. She explained to me that she was only trying to give me a better life. If she could not get into America, she wanted me to get in. I said I didn't want to leave her. I wanted to stay with my mother. Mother hugged me, but I knew she wasn't listening to me. She had made up her mind.

The day came when the woman's family came to Angel Island. I remember Mother holding me as long as she could before letting me go. For days, they trained me to follow their plan. They made sure that I would call the stranger Mother. If I made a mistake, I could ruin the plan for both the stranger and me. I was confused and frightened. I had to think of her now as my mother. It wasn't just for the test, either. If we did pass, she would have to be my new mother in America.

I remember walking out of the cell. I remember turning around. My mother waved and smiled at me. There were tears in her eyes. She then turned around and disappeared into the crowd of women in the cell. I was sure that would be the last time I would ever see my mother.

I walked out with the stranger, my new mother. We were brought into a room. Her family was inside. She was lucky. Her family had come for her from San Francisco. An immigration man was also in the room. He looked like a nice man. A translator sat next to him. They looked closely at both of us.

The interview began. The immigration man and the translator asked the strange woman many questions about her family. I remember that her family was also talking. They were Chinese, but they were speaking in English. I thought it was funny to hear them talk English. I had never really heard a Chinese person speak it before.

The translator would still translate for the stranger, though. It was his job. They didn't want to rely on her family to translate. I remember that the immigration man smiled at me. He seemed to like me. I don't mean to brag, but I am told I was a very cute little girl (just like you are now, my granddaughter). He smiled at me and pinched my cheek. I think I laughed at him. It seemed to make him happy. I remember he had a hairy face, which I was not used to. He still seemed like a nice man, though.

Then, he asked me a question about my mother. Just as we had practiced days before, I turned to the stranger and hugged her. This was the only question he asked me. The immigration man smiled and started speaking in English to the stranger's family. They were happy with the words he said. He took the stranger's papers and stamped them. We had passed. We were allowed into America.

Just as everyone was about to leave the room, I started crying. I don't know why, really. I think I knew what it all meant now. I remember looking at the stranger. I didn't like her face. I looked at her family. I didn't like the way they looked either. I started crying more and more. The stranger picked me up and tried to stop me. The tighter she held me, the more I cried. I started yelling in Chinese. I said I wanted my mother.

I remember the stranger started to cover my mouth. I bit her and kept crying for my mother. I knew then that I couldn't live with the stranger. I wanted my mother. I remember seeing the stranger's family. They were all looking at me with angry faces. The immigration man wanted to know what I was crying about. I was about to ruin it for everyone.

The translator said something. The immigration man looked confused. They exchanged a few words. I remember the officer walking out of the room. I remember everyone looked scared.

While he was gone, I heard the translator talking to the stranger and her family in Chinese. I listened. He told them that he had guessed what was really going on, but he had not told the immigration man. He knew I wasn't the stranger's baby. He had guessed that even before I started crying for my mother.

The translator said he was tired of all the bad things that had been happening to the Chinese on Angel Island. He had seen many families broken up and decided that he couldn't allow it anymore. Translating was his job. He needed that to live. But he also could not allow wrong things to happen to innocent people. He was ashamed at how his country had been treating all the Chinese people. He knew that they only wanted to have a chance at a better life.

He had told the immigration man that I had been crying for my nanny. He knew the immigration man well enough. He knew that the officer had a weakness for cute children. When the immigration man heard that I was calling for my nanny, he asked for her. The translator told him that she was still in the cell. He really meant my mother.

The immigration man came back in. He picked me up and brought me to the cells. The translator asked me to point at my mother. I remember she was crying. I think she was afraid for me. The translator told me to point again, so I did. Before I knew it, my mother was out of the cell and walking back to the other place with us. I stopped crying as soon as she held me again.

The translator explained quickly to mother that, if she wanted to be able to enter America with me, she had to pretend to be my nanny. Mother understood. She gave me a quick hug.

It was lucky the immigration man did not know how to speak Chinese. If he had, I wouldn't be here. Neither would you, granddaughter. It was also lucky that he had a soft heart for cute children.

We went back into the room where the stranger and her family were. Mother pretended she was my nanny. The immigration man told us, through the translator, that he had a baby, too. He said he considered his nanny a part of his family. Even though it was not quite the rule, he would allow my nanny (my mother) to enter America with us. He hated to see little girls cry. He pinched my checks again.

Mother grabbed me. I remember I smiled. The immigration man smiled back. The translator did, too. Before I knew it, we were on the ferry. Angel Island was behind us and America was in front of us. We were going to make it after all.

That's how we got into America, Granddaughter. We owe much to luck, as well as the kindness of strangers. We owe much to the people who had family in San Francisco. We owe much to that translator on Angel Island. I suppose there was at least one true angel on that island. But it was close. I almost lost my mother.

When you come, we will go to Angel Island. That awful immigration station is closed now. When we go there with your mother, I will take you both to the places I mentioned. I will show you the building where my mother and I were trapped. I will show you the walls where even now some of the poetry remains. Because you do not speak Chinese, I will translate for you.

These things really happened. They happened to many Chinese who came to this country. Many were lucky, like we were. But many were not. Angel Island is a monument to all of us who suffered and struggled to come to the United States.

So now you know the beginning. There is much more of our story to tell. But I will save that for when you arrive here. I will be waiting for you at the airport with a hug.

See you soon, my dearest granddaughter.

Love,
Grandma

Thinking About It

1. Which Chinese people were being let into the United States? Which were being sent back to China?

2. Why was the translator so helpful?

3. Why do you think the great-grandmother wants her great-granddaugher to know about her experiences on Angel Island?